Tucholsky Wagner Zola Scott Sydow Fonatne Freud Schlegel
Turgenev Wallace
Twain Walther von der Vogelweide Fouqué Friedrich II. von Preußen
Weber Freiligrath Frey
Fechner Fichte Weiße Rose von Fallersleben Kant Ernst Richthofen Frommel
Engels Fielding Hölderlin
Fehrs Faber Flaubert Eichendorff Tacitus Dumas
Maximilian I. von Habsburg Fock Eliasberg Zweig Ebner Eschenbach
Feuerbach Ewald Eliot Vergil
Goethe Elisabeth von Österreich London
Mendelssohn Balzac Shakespeare Dostojewski Ganghofer
Trackl Stevenson Lichtenberg Rathenau Doyle Gjellerup
Mommsen Tolstoi Hambruch
Thoma Lenz Hanrieder Droste-Hülshoff
Dach Verne von Arnim Hägele Hauff Humboldt
Reuter
Karrillon Garschin Rousseau Hagen Hauptmann Gautier
Damaschke Defoe Hebbel Baudelaire
Descartes
Wolfram von Eschenbach Schopenhauer Hegel Kussmaul Herder
Bronner Darwin Melville Dickens Grimm Jerome Rilke George
Campe Horváth Aristoteles Bebel Proust
Bismarck Vigny Gengenbach Barlach Voltaire Federer Herodot
Heine
Storm Casanova Tersteegen Gilm Grillparzer Georgy
Chamberlain Lessing Langbein Gryphius
Brentano Lafontaine
Strachwitz Claudius Schiller Kralik Iffland Sokrates
Bellamy Schilling
Katharina II. von Rußland Gerstäcker Raabe Gibbon Tschechow
Löns Hesse Hoffmann Gogol Wilde Gleim Vulpius
Luther Heym Hofmannsthal Klee Hölty Morgenstern Goedicke
Roth Heyse Klopstock Kleist
Luxemburg Puschkin Homer Mörike
La Roche Horaz Musil
Machiavelli Kraft Kraus
Navarra Aurel Musset Kierkegaard
Lamprecht Kind Kirchhoff Hugo Moltke
Nestroy Marie de France
Nietzsche Nansen Laotse Ipsen Liebknecht
Marx Ringelnatz
von Ossietzky Lassalle Gorki Klett Leibniz
May vom Stein Lawrence Irving
Petalozzi Platon Knigge
Sachs Poe Pückler Michelangelo Kock Kafka
Liebermann Korolenko
de Sade Praetorius Mistral Zetkin

# For Auld Lang Syne

Ray Woodward

# Imprint

This book is part of the TREDITION CLASSICS series.

Author: Ray Woodward
Cover design: toepferschumann, Berlin (Germany)

Publisher: tredition GmbH, Hamburg (Germany)
ISBN: 978-3-8491-4790-7

www.tredition.com
www.tredition.de

# For Auld Lang Syne

## A Book Of Friendship

Selected
by
RAY WOODWARD

*Affectionately Dedicated to*

My Father,
FRED E. WOODWARD.

# INTRODUCTION

Friendship is essentially the same bond, whether it unites persons of intellect and refined tastes, or those more unfortunate ones, who, perhaps, have no conception of their mission in the world, or of their duty to society. Its manifestations may be wholly different, but the two friendships will have some points in common. In both instances the friends are drawn close together and are united by that bond which has been so beautifully written about throughout the ages.

The abstract theorizing of one philosopher can never satisfy the individual in regard to the varied manifestations of friendship, and it is therefore interesting and profitable to note what various writers have said about this world-wide force under the varying conditions of the past and the present. It would be a well-nigh hopeless task to attempt to gather within the compass of a single volume all that has been written about it. The present volume present some selections that express in a measure what is implied by the word Friendship.

## For Auld Lang Syne

It is a noble and great thing to cover the blemishes and to excuse the failings of a friend; to draw a curtain before his stains, and to display his perfections; to bury his weaknesses in silence, but to proclaim his virtues upon the housetop.

—*South.*

* * * * *

E'en as a traveller, meeting with the shade
Of some o'erhanging tree, awhile reposes,
Then leaves its shelter to pursue his way,
So men meet friends, then part with them forever.

—*Hitopadesa.*

* * * * *

A true friendship is as wise as it is tender.

—*Thoreau.*

* * * * *

As ships meet at sea—a moment together, when words of greeting must be spoken, and then away upon the deep—so men meet in this world; and I think we should cross no man's path without hailing him, and if he needs, giving him supplies.

—*H. W. Beecher.*

* * * * *

A friend is more necessary than either fire or water.

—*Proverbs.*

* * * * *

A long novitiate of acquaintance should precede the vows of friendship.

—*Lord Bolingbroke.*

* * * * *

A beloved friend does not fill one part of the soul, but, penetrating the whole, becomes connected with all feeling.

—*Channing.*

* * * * *

A reverse of fortune is a mighty sifter of friendship. So is distance. Go a little way out of town, and see how many people will take the trouble to come to see you. Well, we must be patient and forbearing. It is a question of intensity of need. Friendly relations depend upon vicinity amongst other things, and there are degrees; but the best kind of friendship has a way of bridging time and space for all that.

—*Haweis.*

* * * * *

A female friend, amiable, clever, and devoted, is a possession more valuable than parks and palaces; and without such a muse few men can succeed in life, none be contented.

—*Lord Beaconsfield.*

* * * * *

A true friend embraces our objects as his own. We feel another mind bent on the same end, enjoying it, ensuring it, reflecting it, and delighting in our devotion to it.

—*Channing.*

* * * * *

A pretended affection is not easily distinguished from a real one, unless in seasons of distress. For adversity is to friendship what fire is to gold—the only infallible test to discover the genuine from the counterfeit. In all other cases they both have the same common marks.

—*Cicero.*

* * * * *

A little peaceful home bounds all my wants and wishes;
Add to this my book and friend—and this is happiness supreme.

—*Montaigne.*

* * * * *

A true friend is more precious to the soul than all which it inherits beneath the sun.

—*Irving.*

* * * * *

A friend
Welded into our life is more to us
Than twice five-thousand kinsmen, one in blood.

—*Euripides.*

* * * * *

A principal fruit of friendship is the ease and discharge of the fullness and swelling of the heart, which passions of all kinds do cause and induce. No receipt openeth the heart but a true friend, to whom you may impart griefs, joys, fears, hopes, suspicions, counsels, and whatsoever lieth upon the heart to oppress it, in a kind of civil shrift or confession.

—*Bacon.*

* * * * *

Be true to thy friend. Never speak of his faults to another, to show thy own discrimination; but open them all to him, with candor and true gentleness; forgive all his errors and his sins, be they ever so many; but do not excuse the slightest deviation from rectitude. Never forbear to dissent from a false opinion, or a wrong practice, from mistaken motives of kindness; nor seek thus to have thy own weaknesses sustained; for these things cannot be done without injury to the soul.

—*Child.*

* * * * *

Be admonished not to strike leagues of friendship with cheap persons, where no friendship can be.

—*Emerson.*

* * * * *

A day for toil, an hour for sport,
But for a friend life is too short.

—*Emerson.*

* * * * *

After a certain age a new friend is a wonder. There is the age of blossoms and sweet budding green, the age of generous summer, the autumn when the leaves drop, and then winter shivering and bare.

—*Thackeray.*

* * * * *

Bitter and unrelenting enemies often deserve better of us than those friends whom we are inclined to regard as pleasant companions; the former often tell us the truth, the latter never.

—*Cicero.*

* * * * *

Does friendship really go on to be more pain than pleasure? I doubt it, for even in its deepest sorrows there is a joy which makes ordinary pleasure a very poor, meaningless affair.

—*Unknown.*

* * * * *

Friendship does not spring up and grow great and become perfect all at once, but requires time and the nourishment of thoughts.

—*Dante.*

* * * * *

Even the utmost good-will and harmony and practical kindness are not sufficient for friendship, for friends do not live in harmony, merely, as some say, but in melody. We do not wish for friends to feed and clothe our bodies,—neighbors are kind enough for that,—but to do the like office to our spirits. For this, few are rich enough, however well disposed they may be.

—*Thoreau*.

*****

A pure friendship inspires, cleanses, expands, and strengthens the soul.

—*Alger*.

*****

A friend is he that loves, and he that is beloved.

—*Hobbe*.

*****

Change, care, nor Time while life endure
Shall spoil our ancient friendship sure.

—*Lang*.

*****

Every young man is the better for cherishing strong friendships with the wise and good; and he whose soul is knit to one or more chosen associates with whom he can sympathize in right aims and feelings, is thereby the better armed against temptation and confirmed in paths of virtue.

—*Carlyle*.

*****

Believing hear, what you deserve to hear:
Your birthday, as my own, to me is dear.
Blest and distinguished days! which we should prize
The first, the kindest, bounty of the skies.
But yours gives most; for mine did only lend
Me to the world, yours gave to me a friend.

*—Martial.*

* * * * *

Choose for your friend him that is wise and good, and secret and just, ingenious and honest, and in those things which have a latitude, use your own liberty.

*—Taylor.*

* * * * *

Friendship is made up of esteem and pleasure; pity is composed of sorrow and contempt: the mind may for some time fluctuate between them, but it can never entertain both at once.

*—Goldsmith.*

* * * * *

Friends are much better tried in bad fortune than in good fortune.

*—Aristotle.*

* * * * *

Fellowship of souls does not consist in the proximity of persons. There are millions who live in close personal contact—dwell under the same roof, board at the same table, and work in the same shop—between whose minds there is scarcely a point of contact, whose souls are as far asunder as the poles; whilst, contrariwise, there are those separated by oceans and continents, ay, by the mysterious gulf that divides time from eternity, between whom there is a constant intercourse, a delightful fellowship. In truth, we have often more communion with the distant than the near.

*—Dr. Thomas.*

* * * * *

Friendship must live by faith and not by sight.

*—Eliot.*

* * * * *

Friends should not be chosen to flatter. The quality we should prize is that rectitude which will shrink from no truth. Intimacies, which increase vanity, destroy friendship.

—*Channing.*

* * * * *

Favors, and especially pecuniary ones, are generally fatal to friendship; for our pride will ever prompt us to lower the value of the gift by diminishing that of the donor. Ingratitude is an effort to recover our own esteem by getting rid of our esteem for our benefactor, whom we look upon as a sort of tooth-drawer, that has cured us of one pain by inflicting another.

—*Smith.*

* * * * *

Friendship throws a greater lustre on prosperity, while it lightens adversity by sharing in its griefs and anxieties.

—*Cicero.*

* * * * *

Friendship hath the skill and observation of the best physician; the diligence and vigilance of the best nurse; and the tenderness and patience of the best mother.

—*Lord Clarendon.*

* * * * *

Friendship! the precious gold of life
By age refined, yet ever new;
Tried in the crucible of time
It always rings of service true.

Friendship! the beauteous soul of life
Which gladdens youth and strengthens age;
May it our hearts and lives entwine
Together on life's fleeting page.

—*Shaylor.*

* * * * *

Friendship is the shadow of the evening, which strengthens with the setting sun of life.

—*La Fontaine.*

* * * * *

Friendship, love, and piety, ought to be handled with a sort of mysterious secrecy; they ought to be spoken of only in the rare moments of perfect confidence.

—*Novalis.*

* * * * *

Few men are calculated for that close connection which we distinguish by the name of friendship, and we well know the difference between a friend and an acquaintance.

—*Sterne.*

* * * * *

Friendship is the nearest thing we know to what religion is. God is love. And to make religion akin to friendship is simply to give it the highest expression conceivable by man.

—*Drummond.*

* * * * *

Friendship is the great chain of human society.

—*Howell.*

* * * * *

Friendship is an allay of our sorrows, the ease of our passions, the discharge of our oppressions, the sanctuary to our calamities, the counsellor of our doubts, the charity of our minds, the emission of our thoughts, the exercise and improvement of what we meditate.

—*Taylor.*

* * * * *

Friendship springs up from sources so subtile and undefinable, that it cannot be *forced* into particular channels; and whenever the attempt has been made, it has usually been unsuccessful.

—*Day.*

* * * * *

God wills that we have sorrows here,
And we will share it;
Whisper thy sorrow in my ear,
That I may also bear it.
If anywhere our trouble seems
To find an end,
'Tis in the fairy land of dreams,
Or with a friend.

—*Tennyson.*

*****

Friendship is a union of spirits, a marriage of hearts, and the bond thereof virtue.

—*Penn.*

*****

Friendship that makes the least noise is very often the most useful; for which reason I should prefer a prudent friend to a zealous one.

—*Addison.*

*****

Friendship, like love, is but a name
Unless to one you stint the flame.
The child, whom many fathers share,
Hath seldom known a father's care.
'Tis thus in friendships; who depends
On many, rarely finds a friend.

—*Gay.*

*****

Friend is a word of royal tone;
Friend is a poem all alone.

—*From the Persian.*

*****

Get not your friends by bare compliments, but by giving them sensible tokens of your love. It is well worth while to learn how to win the heart of man the right way. Force is of no use to make or preserve a friend, who is an animal that is never caught and tamed but by kindness and pleasure. Excite them by your civilities, and show them that you desire nothing more than their satisfaction; oblige with all your soul that friend who has made you a present of his own.

—*Socrates.*

*****

He who gives pleasure, meets with it; kindness is the bond of friendship, and the book of love; he who sows not, reaps not.

*****

Friendship is the holiest of gifts,
God can bestow nothing more sacred upon us!
It enhances every joy, mitigates every pain.
Everyone can have a friend
Who himself knows how to be a friend.

—*Teidge.*

*****

In this respect friendship is superior to relationship, because from relationship benevolence can be withdrawn, and from friendship it cannot; for with the withdrawal of benevolence the very name of friendship is done away, while that of relationship remains.

—*Cicero.*

*****

I want a warm and faithful friend,
To cheer the adverse hour;
Who ne'er to flatter will descend,
Nor bend the knee to power.
A friend to chide me when I'm wrong,
My inmost soul to see;

And that my friendship prove as strong
To him as his to me.

—*Adams.*

* * * * *

Friendship's true laws are by this rule expressed,
Welcome the coming, speed the parting guest.

—*Pope.*

* * * * *

Human spirits are only to be drawn together and held together by the living bond of having found something in which they really do agree.

—*Greenwell.*

* * * * *

He has the substance of all bliss
To whom a virtuous friend is given:
So sweet harmonious friendship is,
Add but eternity, you'll make it heaven.

—*Norris.*

* * * * *

He who wrongs his friend
Wrongs himself more and ever bears about
A silent court of justice in his breast.

—*Tennyson.*

* * * * *

Hearts only thrive on varied good,
And he who gathers from a host
Of friendly hearts his daily food,
Is the best friend that we can boast.

—*Holland.*

* * * * *

I exhort you to lay the foundations of virtue, without which friendship cannot exist, in such a manner that, with this one exception, you may consider that nothing in the world is more excellent than friendship.

—*Cicero.*

* * * * *

It is a beautiful thing to feel that our friends are God's gifts to us. Thinking of it has made me understand why we love and are loved, sometimes when we cannot explain what causes the feeling. Feeling so makes friendship such a sacred, holy thing!

—*Porter.*

* * * * *

If my brother, or kinsman, will be my friend, I ought to prefer him before a stranger; or I show little duty or nature to my parents.

And as we ought to prefer our kindred in point of affection, so, too, in point of charity, if equally needing and deserving.

—*Penn.*

* * * * *

It is equally impossible to forget our friends, and to make them answer to our ideal. When they say farewell, then indeed we begin to keep them company. How often we find ourselves turning our backs on our actual friends that we may go out and meet their ideal cousins!

—*Thoreau.*

* * * * *

I must feel pride in my friend's accomplishments as if they were mine—wild, delicate, throbbing property in his virtues. I feel as warmly when he is praised as the lover when he hears applause of his engaged maiden.

—*Emerson.*

* * * * *

In very many cases of friendship, or what passes for it, the old axiom is reversed, and like clings to unlike more than to like.

—*Dickens.*

* * * * *

Hearts are linked to hearts by God. The friend on whose fidelity you can count, whose success in life flushes your cheek with honest satisfaction, whose triumphant career you have traced and read with a heart throbbing almost as if it were a thing alive, for whose honor you would answer as for your own; that friend, given to you by circumstances over which you have no control, was God's own gift.

—*Robertson.*

* * * * *

If thou neglect thy love to thy neighbor, in vain thou professest thy love to God.

—*Quarles.*

* * * * *

I cannot contentedly frame a prayer for myself in particular, without a catalogue for my friends; nor request a happiness, wherein my sociable disposition doth not desire the fellowship of my neighbor.

—*Browne.*

* * * * *

It's an owercome sooth for age an' youth
  And it brooks wi' nae denial,
That the dearest friends are the auldest friends
  And the young are just on trial.

There's a rival bauld wi' young an' auld
  And it's him that has bereft me;
For the surest friends are the auldest friends

And the maist o' mine hae left me.

There are kind hearts still, for friends to fill
And fools to take and break them;
But the nearest friends are the auldest friends
And the grave's the place to seek them.

—*Stevenson.*

* * * * *

God divided man into men that they might help each other.

—*Seneca.*

* * * * *

I sometimes hear my friends complain finely that I do not appreciate their fineness. I shall not tell them whether I do or not. As if they expected a vote of thanks for every fine thing which they uttered or did! Who knows but it was finely appreciated? It may be that your silence was the finer thing of the two.... In human intercourse the tragedy begins, not when there is misunderstanding about words, but when silence is not understood. Then there can never be an explanation.

—*Thoreau.*

* * * * *

It is a friendly heart that has plenty of friends.

—*Thackeray.*

* * * * *

It is not becoming to turn from friends in adversity, but then it is for those who have basked in the sunshine of their prosperity to adhere to them. No one was ever so foolish as to select the unfortunate for their friends.

—*Lucanus.*

* * * * *

It is essential to friendship that there be no labor to pass for more than we are, no effort, no anxiety to hide! If anything be concealed, the constant intercourse of friends will discover it, and one discovery will produce others. The idea that the heart has one secret fold extinguishes affection.

—*Channing*.

* * * * *

Impatient and uncertain lovers think that they must say or do something kind whenever they meet; they must never be cold. But they who are friends do not do what they think they must, but what they must. Even their friendship is, in one sense, a sublime phenomenon to them.

—*Thoreau*.

* * * * *

It is a good and safe rule to sojourn in many places, as if you meant to spend your life there, never omitting an opportunity of doing a kindness or speaking a true word or making a friend.

—*Ruskin*.

* * * * *

It has seemed to me lately more possible than I knew, to carry a friendship greatly, on one side, without due correspondence on the other. Why should I cumber myself with the poor fact that the receiver is not capacious? It never troubles the sun that some of his rays fall wide and vain into ungrateful space, and only a small part on the reflecting planet.... It is thought a disgrace to love unrequited. But the great will see that true love cannot be unrequited.

—*Emerson*.

* * * * *

In the cause of friendship brave all dangers.

—*Dickens*.

* * * * *

Kindness given and received aright and knitting two hearts into one is a thing of heaven, as rare in this world as a perfect love; both are the overflow of only very rare and beautiful souls.

—*Balzac.*

* * * * *

Kindred passions and pursuits are the natural groundwork of friendship. Real friendship is of slow growth, and never thrives, unless ingrafted upon a stock of known and reciprocal merit.

—*Chesterfield.*

* * * * *

Let this, therefore, be established as a primary law concerning friendship, that we expect from our friends only what is honorable, and for our friends' sake do what is honorable; that we should not wait till we are asked; that zeal be ever ready, and reluctance far from us.

—*Cicero.*

* * * * *

Let Friendship's accents cheer our doubtful way,
And Love's pure planet lend its guiding ray,—
Our tardy Art shall wear an angel's wings,
And life shall lengthen with the joy it brings!

—*Holmes.*

* * * * *

I am not of that feather, to shake off my friend when most he needs me.

—*Shakespeare.*

* * * * *

Let the honor of thy friend be as dear unto thee as thy own.

—*The Talmud.*

* * * * *

Life to be rich and fertile must be reinforced with friendship. It is the sap that preserves from blight and withering; it is the sunshine that beckons on the blossoming and fruitage; it is the starlight dew that perfumes life with sweetness and besprinkles it with splendor;

it is the music-tide that sweeps the soul, scattering treasures; it is the victorious and blessed leader of integrity's forlorn hope; it is the potent alchemy that transmutes failure into success; it is the hidden manna that nourishes when all other sustenance fails; it is the voice that speaks to hopes all dead, "Because I live, ye shall live also." For the loftiest friendships have no commercial element in them: they are founded on disinterestedness and sacrifices. They neither expect nor desire a return for gift or service. Amid the tireless breaking of the billows on the shores of experience, there is no surer anchorage than a friendship that "beareth all things, believeth all things, hopeth all things."

—*Cooper.*

* * * * *

It is one of the wretchednesses of the great that they have no approved friends. Kings are the most solitary beings on earth.

—*Channing.*

* * * * *

Many kinds of fruit grow upon the tree of life, but none so sweet as friendship.

—*Larcom.*

* * * * *

My treasures are my friends.

—*Constantius.*

* * * * *

Life should be fortified by many friendships.

—*Smith.*

* * * * *

Love begins with love; and there is no passing from firm friendship to even feeble love.

—*La Bruyere.*

* * * * *

Live not without a friend; the Alpine rock must own
Its mossy grace or else be nothing but a stone.

—*Story.*

*****

Let the soul be assured that somewhere in the universe it should rejoin its friend, and it would be content and cheerful alone for a thousand years.

—*Emerson.*

*****

Make new friends, but keep the old;
Those are silver, these are gold,
Brow may wrinkle, hair grows grey:
True friendship never knows decay.

—*Anon.*

*****

Oh, the comfort—the inexpressible comfort of feeling safe with a person—having neither to weigh thought nor measure words, but pouring them all right out, just as they are, chaff and grain together; certain that a faithful hand will take and sift them, keep what is worth keeping, and with the breath of kindness blow the rest away.

—*Muloch.*

*****

O matchless wisdom; those seem to take the sun out of the world who remove friendship from the pleasures of life: than which we have received nothing better or more pleasant from the gods.

—*Cicero.*

*****

Not on the store of sprightly wine,
  Nor plenty of delicious meats,
Though generous Nature did design
  To court us with perpetual treats;

'Tis not on these we for content depend,
So much as on the shadow of a friend.

—*Menander.*

*****

Since human affairs are frail and fleeting, some persons must ever be sought for whom we may love, and by whom we may be loved; for when affection and kind feeling are done away with, all cheerfulness likewise is banished from existence.

—*Cicero.*

*****

Lying on lower levels is but a trivial offence compared with civility and compliments on the level of friendship.

—*Thoreau.*

*****

My friend, with you to live alone,
Were how much better than to own
A crown, a sceptre and a throne!

—*Tennyson.*

*****

Pure friendship is something which men of an inferior intellect can never taste.

—*La Bruyere.*

*****

Sweet words will multiply a man's friends; and a fair-speaking tongue will multiply courtesies. Let those that are at peace with thee be many; but thy counsellors one of a thousand. If thou wouldest get thee a friend, get him by proving, and be not in haste to trust him. For there is a friend that is so for his own occasion, and he will not continue in the day of thy affliction. And there is a friend that turneth to enmity; and he will discover strife to thy reproach. And there is a friend that is a companion at the table, and he will not continue in the day of thy affliction; and in thy prosperity he will be as thyself, and will be bold over thy servants; if thou shalt be brought low, he will be against thee, and he will hide himself from thy face.

—*Bible.*

* * * * *

The first thing you should procure, after faith, is a good friend.

—*Arabic.*

* * * * *

Such a friendship, that through it we love places and seasons; for as bright bodies emit rays at a distance, and flowers drop their sweet leaves on the ground around them, so friends impart favor even to the places where they dwell. With friends even poverty is pleasant. Words cannot express the joy which a friend imparts; they only can know who have experienced. A friend is dearer than the light of heaven, for it would be better for us that the sun were extinguished than that we should be without friends.

—*S. Chrysostom.*

* * * * *

Strange as it may sound, we are sometimes rather disposed to choose our friends from the unworthy than the worthy; for though it is difficult to love those whom we do not esteem, it is a greater difficulty to love those whom we esteem much more than ourselves. A perfect friendship requires equality, even in virtue.

—*Smith.*

* * * * *

Sincerity, truth, faithfulness, come into the very essence of friendship.

—*Channing.*

* * * * *

Somehow or other, friendship entwines itself with the life of all men, nor does it suffer any mode of spending our life to be independent of itself.

—*Cicero.*

* * * * *

Small service is true service while it lasts,
Of humblest friends, bright creature, scorn not one;
The daisy by the shadow that it casts
Protects the lingering dewdrop from the sun.

—*Wordsworth.*

* * * * *

Some friendships are made by nature, some by contract, some by interest, and some by souls.

—*Taylor.*

* * * * *

They who dare to ask anything of a friend, by their very request seem to imply that they would do anything for the sake of a friend.

—*Cicero.*

* * * * *

To act the part of a true friend requires more conscientious feeling than to fill with credit and complacency any other station or capacity in social life.

—*Ellis.*

* * * * *

There is as much difference between the counsel that a friend giveth and that a man giveth himself, as there is between the counsel of a friend and of a flatterer. For there is no such flatterer as is a man's self; and there is no such remedy against flattery of a man's self as the liberty of a friend.

—*Bacon.*

* * * * *

The laws of friendship are austere and eternal, of one web with the laws of nature and of morals.

—*Emerson.*

*****

To he only an admirer is not to be a friend of a human being. Human nature wants something more, and our perceptions are diseased when we dress up a human being in the attributes of divinity. He is our friend who loves more than admires us, and would aid us in our great work.

—*Channing.*

*****

True, active, productive friendship consists in keeping equal pace in life, in the approval of my aims by my friend, while I approve his, and thus moving forward together steadily, however much our way of thought and life may vary.

—*Goethe.*

*****

The man, that comforts a desponding friend
With words alone, does nothing. He's a friend
Indeed, who proves himself a friend in need.

—*Plautus.*

*****

The making of friends, who are real friends, is the best token we have of a man's success in life.

—*Hale.*

*****

Truthfulness, frankness, disinterestedness, and faithfulness are the qualities absolutely essential to friendship, and these must be crowned by a sympathy that enters into all the joys, the sorrows and the interests of the friend; that delights in all his upward progress, and when he stumbles or falls, stretches out the helping hand, and is tender and patient even when it condemns.

—*Ware.*

* * * * *

The expensiveness of friendship does not lie in what one does for one's friends, but in what, out of regard for them, one leaves undone.

—*Ibsen.*

* * * * *

There are three friendships which are advantageous, and three which are injurious. Friendship with the upright; friendship with the sincere; and friendship with the man of observation: these are advantageous. Friendship with the man of specious airs; friendship with the insinuatingly soft; and friendship with the glib-tongued: these are injurious.

—*Confucius.*

* * * * *

The tree withereth
Which stands in the courtyard
Without shelter of bark or of leaf.
So is a man
Destitute of friends.
Why should he live on?

—*The Hava-mal.*

* * * * *

There is nothing that is meritorious but virtue and friendship, and indeed, friendship itself is but a part of virtue.

—*Pope.*

* * * * *

The mind never unbends itself so agreeably as in the conversation of a well-chosen friend. There is indeed no blessing of life that is any way comparable to the enjoyment of a discreet and virtuous friend. It eases and unloads the mind, clears and improves the understanding, engenders thoughts and knowledge, animates virtue and good resolutions, soothes and allays the passions, and finds employment for most of the vacant hours of life.

—*Addison.*

* * * * *

The best way to represent to life the manifold use of friendship is to cast and see how many things there are which a man cannot do himself;
and then it will appear that it was a sparing speech of the ancients to
say "that a friend is another himself."

—*Bacon.*

* * * * *

The conversation of a friend brightens the eyes.

—*Persian Proverb.*

* * * * *

Those who want friends to open themselves unto, are cannibals of their own hearts. But one thing is most admirable, which is, that this communicating of a man's self to his friend works two contrary effects; for it redoubleth joys, and cutteth grief in halfs. For there is no man that imparteth his joys to his friends, but he joyeth the more; and no man that imparteth his griefs to his friend, but he grieveth the less.

—*Bacon.*

* * * * *

There is no better medicine for grief than the advice of a good and honored friend. He who, in his sufferings, excites and tries to soothe his mind by wine, though he may have pleasure for a moment, has a double portion of pain afterwards.

—*Euripides.*

* * * * *

Time draweth wrinkles in a fair face, but addeth fresh colors to a fast friend.

—*Lyle.*

* * * * *

The good man has the same relation to his friend as he has to himself.

—*Aristotle.*

* * * * *

There is in friendship something of all relations and something above them all. It is the golden thread that ties the hearts of all the world.

—*Evelyn.*

* * * * *

To God be humble, and to thy friend be kind.

—*Dunbar.*

* * * * *

The perfection of loving-kindness is to efface ourselves so thoroughly that those we benefit shall not think themselves inferior to him who benefits them.

—*Balzac.*

* * * * *

The purest and most lasting human friendships are permeated with an element of reverence.

—*Phelps.*

* * * * *

There are gold-bright suns in worlds above,
And blazing gems in worlds below,
Our world has Love and only Love,
For living warmth and jewel glow;
God's love is sunlight to the good,
And Woman's pure as diamond sheen,
And Friendships's mystic brotherhood
In twilight beauty lies between.

—*Milne.*

* * * * *

The friendship which arises from contraries is horrible and coarse, and has often no tie of communion; but that which arises from likeness is gentle, and has a tie of communion, which lasts through life.

—*Plato.*

* * * * *

To live with one's enemies as if they might one day be our friends, and to live with our friends as though they might one day become our enemies, is neither natural to hatred nor consistent with friendship. Such a maxim is not moral, but politic.

—*La Bruyere.*

* * * * *

To take the companionship of life from life, what else is it than to take away the means of absent friends conversing together?

—*Cicero.*

* * * * *

The love of friendship is the most perfect form of loving.

—*Cardinal Manning.*

* * * * *

The highest compact we can make with our fellow is, Let there be truth between us two forevermore. It is sublime to feel and say of another, I need never meet, or speak, or write to him; we need not reinforce ourselves or send tokens of remembrance, I rely on him as on myself; if he did thus or thus I know it was right.

—*Emerson.*

* * * * *

True friendship between man and man is infinite and immortal.

—*Plato.*

* * * * *

There is a magic in the memory of schoolboy friendships; it softens the heart, and even affects the nervous system of those who have no hearts.

—*Disraeli.*

* * * * *

Think it not friendship which ever seeks itself, but that which gives itself for others.

—*Marshall.*

* * * * *

The vital air of friendship is composed of confidences.

—*Roux.*

* * * * *

When Socrates was building himself a house at Athens, being asked by one that observed the littleness of the design why a man so eminent would not have an abode more suitable to his dignity, he replied that he should think himself sufficiently accommodated if he could see that narrow habitation filled with real friends.

—*Johnson.*

* * * * *

While friendship embraces very many and great advantages, she undoubtedly surpasses all in this, that she shines with a brilliant hope over the future, and never suffers the spirit to be weakened or to sink. Besides, he who looks on a true friend, looks, as it were, upon a kind of image of himself; wherefore, friends, though absent, are still present; though in poverty, they are rich; though weak, yet in the enjoyment of health; and, what is still more difficult to assert, though dead, they are alive; so entirely does the honor, the memory, the regret of friends attend them.

—*Cicero.*

* * * * *

Thine own friend and thy father's friend, forsake not.

—*Solomon.*

* * * * *

While I keep my senses I shall prefer nothing to a pleasant friend.

—*Horace.*

* * * * *

What a great blessing is a friend, with a breast so trusty that thou mayest safely bury all thy secrets in it, whose conscience thou mayest fear less than thine own, who can relieve thy cares by his conversation, thy doubts by his counsels, thy sadness by his good humor, and whose very look gives comfort to thee!

—*Seneca.*

* * * * *

What can be more delightful than to have one to whom you can speak on all subjects just as to yourself? Where would be the great enjoyment in prosperity if you had not one to rejoice in it equally with yourself? And adversity would indeed be difficult to endure without some one who would bear it even with greater regret than yourself.

—*Cicero.*

* * * * *

With one friend I would count myself rich.

—*Nusbaum.*

* * * * *

What is bestowed on our friends is beyond the reach of fortune; the riches that thou hast given away are the only riches that thou really possessest.

—*Martial.*

* * * * *

Well chosen friendship, the most noble
Of virtues, all our joys makes double
And into halves divides our trouble.

—*Denham.*

* * * * *

We are most of us very lonely in this world; you who have any who love you, cling to them and thank God.

—*Thackeray.*

When to the sessions of sweet silent thought
I summon up remembrance of things past,
I sigh the lack of many a thing I sought,
And with old woes new wail my dear time's waste:
Then can I drown an eye, unused to flow,
For precious friends hid in death's dateless night,
And weep afresh love's long since canceled woe,
And moan the expense of many a vanished sight:
Then can I grieve at grievances foregone,
And heavily from woe to woe tell o'er
The sad account of fore-bemoaned moan,
Which I new pay as if not paid before.
But if the while I think on thee, dear friend,
All losses are restored and sorrows end.

—*Shakespeare.*

* * * * *

You shall perceive how you
Mistake my fortunes; I am wealthy in my friends.

—*Shakespeare.*

* * * * *

You must, therefore, love me myself, and not my circumstances, if we are to be real friends.

—*Cicero.*

* * * * *

With conscious pride I view the band
Of faithful friends that round me stand,
With pride exult that I alone
Can join these scattered gems in one;

For they're a wreath of pearls, and I
The silken cord on which they lie.
'Tis mine their inmost souls to see,
Unlocked is every heart to me,
To me they cling, on me they rest,
And I've a place in every breast.
For they're a wreath of pearls, and I
The silken cord on which they lie.

—*From the Arabic.*

* * * * *

What room can there be for friendship, or who can be a friend to any one whom he does not love for his own sake? And what is loving, from which verb (amo) the very name of friendship (amicitia) is derived, but wishing a certain person to enjoy the greatest possible good fortune, even if none of it accrues to one's self?

—*Cicero.*

* * * * *

What makes us so changeable in our friendships is the difficulty we have in discerning the qualities of the heart, and the ease with which we discern those of the mind.

—*La Rochefoucauld.*

* * * * *

Worldly friendship is profuse in honeyed words, passionate endearments, commendations of beauty, while true friendship speaks a simple honest language.

—*De Sales.*

* * * * *

You cannot find a man who fully loves any living thing, that, dolt and dullard though he be, is not in some spot lovable himself. He gets something from his friends if he had nothing at all before.

—*Brooks.*

* * * * *

We can live without a brother, but not without a friend.

—*German Proverb.*

* * * * *

Whatever is founded on mere carnal love, vanity or frivolity, on such attractions as are purely external, a sweet voice, personal beauty, superficial cleverness or outward show, is unworthy to be called friendship.

—*De Sales.*

* * * * *

You do surely bar the door upon your own liberty, if you deny your griefs to your friend.

—*Shakespeare.*

* * * * *

When a man cannot fitly play his own part, if he have not a friend he may quit the stage.

—*Bacon.*

* * * * *

We want one or two companions of intelligence, probity, and grace, to wear out life with; persons by whom we can measure ourselves, and who shall hold us fast to good sense and virtue.

—*Emerson.*

* * * * *

A crowd is not company, and faces are but a gallery of pictures; and talk but a tinkling cymbal, where there is no love. In a great town friends are scattered, so that there is not that fellowship, for the most part, which is in less neighborhoods. But we may go farther and affirm most truly, that it is a mere and miserable solitude, to want true friends, without which the world is but a wilderness. Whosoever in the frame of his nature and affections is unfit for friendship, he taketh it of the beast, and not from humanity.

—*Francis Bacon.*

* * * * *

And thou, my friend, whose gentle love
Yet thrills my bosom's chords,
How much thy friendship was above
Description's power of words.

—*Lord Byron.*

*****

As friendship must be founded on mutual esteem, it cannot long exist among the vicious. —*Horace Smith.*

*****

A friend is worth all the hazards we can run.

—*Edward Young.*

*****

A true friend is forever a friend.

—*George MacDonald.*

*****

A benevolent man should allow a few faults in himself, to keep his friends in countenance.

—*Benjamin Franklin.*

*****

A slender acquaintance with the world must convince every man that actions, not words, are the true criterion of the attachment of friends.

—*Washington.*

*****

A faithful friend is better than gold—a medicine for misery, an only possession.

—*Burton.*

*****

Blessed are they who have the gift of making friends, for it is one of God's best gifts. It involves many things, but, above all, the power of going out of one's self and seeing and appreciating whatever is noble and loving in another.

—*Hughes.*

* * * * *

Cultivate the friendships of thy youth; it is only in that generous time they are formed.

—*Thackeray.*

* * * * *

Companions I have enough, friends few.

—*Pope.*

* * * * *

Friendship is steady and peaceful; not much jealousy, and no heartburnings. It strengthens with time, and survives the smallpox and a wooden leg. It doubles our joys, divides our griefs, and warms our lives with a steady flame.

—*Reade.*

* * * * *

Friendship above all ties doth bind the heart,
And Faith is Friendship in its noblest part.

—*Earl of Orrey.*

* * * * *

Friendship, peculiar boon of Heaven,
The noble mind's delight and pride,
To men and angels only given,
To all the lower world denied.

—*Samuel Johnson.*

* * * * *

Friendship is a plant which cannot be forced. True friendship is no gourd, springing up in a night and withering in a day.

—*Charlotte Bronte.*

* * * * *

Friendship always benefits, while love sometimes injures.

—*Seneca.*

* * * * *

Friendship heightens all our affections. We, receive all the ardor of our friend in addition to our own. The communication of minds gives to each the fervor of each.

—*Channing.*

* * * * *

Fate, which has ordained that there shall be no friendship among the evil, has also ordained that there shall ever be friendship among the good.

—*Plato.*

* * * * *

False friendship turns to evil desires, upbraidings, slander, deceit, sorrow, confusion and jealousies; but pure friendship is always the same, modest, courteous and loving, knowing no change save an increasingly pure and perfect union.

—*De Sales.*

* * * * *

Friendship is love with understanding. —*Proverb.*

* * * * *

Friendship consists in forgetting what one gives, and remembering what one receives.

—*Dumas.*

* * * * *

Friendship is said to be a plant of tedious growth, its roots composed of tender fibers, nice in their taste, cautious in spreading.

—*Vanbrough.*

* * * * *

Friendship springs from nature rather than from need.

—*Cicero.*

* * * * *

Friendship, a dear balm—
Whose coming is as light and music are
'Mid dissonance and gloom:—a star
Which moves not 'mid the moving heavens alone;
A smile among dark frowns: a beloved light:
A solitude, a refuge, a delight.

—*P. B. Shelley.*

* * * * *

Friendship is the greatest bond in the world.

—*Jeremy Taylor.*

Friendship is love without wings.

—*Byron.*

For as yellow gold is tried by fire, so do moments of adversity prove the strength of friendship. While fortune is friendly and smiles with serene countenance, crowds surround the rich; but when heaven's thunder rolls, they vanish, nor has he one who knows him, though lately encircled by troops of boon companions.

—*Ovid.*

Our best friends have a tincture of jealousy even in their friendship; and when they hear us praised by others, will ascribe it to sinister and interested motives if they can.

—*C. C. Colton.*

* * * * *

For to have the same predilections and the same aversions, that and that alone is the surest bond of friendship.

—*Sallust.*

False friends, like insects in a summer's day,
  Bask in the sunshine, but avoid the shower;
Uncertain visitants, they flee away
  E'en when misfortune's cloud begins to lower.
Into life's bitter cup true friendship drops
  Balsamic sweets to overpower the gall;
True friends, like ivy and the wall it props,
  Both stand together, or together fall.

—*Anonymous.*

He who cannot feel friendship is alike incapable of love. Let a woman beware of the man who owns that he loves no one but herself.

—*Talleyrand.*

* * * * *

How were friendship possible? In mutual devotedness to the Good and True: otherwise impossible; except as armed neutrality or hollow commercial league. A man, be the heavens ever praised, is sufficient for himself; yet were ten men, united in love, capable of being and doing what ten thousand singly would fail. Infinite is the help man can yield to man!

—*Carlyle.*

He that hath gained a friend, hath given hostages to fortune.

—*Shakespeare.*

How often in thy journeyings hast thou made thee instant friends,
Found, to be loved a little while, and lost, to meet no more;
Friends of happy reminiscences, although so transient in their converse,
Liberal, cheerful, and sincere, a crowd of kindly traits.

—*Tupper.*

* * * * *

Heaven forming each on other to depend,
A master, or a servant, or a friend,

Bids each on other for assistance call,
Till one man's weakness grows the strength of all.

—*Pope.*

In friendship we find nothing false or insincere; everything is straightforward, and springs from the heart.

—*Cicero.*

Keep well thine tongue and keep thy friend.

—*Chaucer.*

Thy friend will come to thee unsought,
With nothing can his love be bought,
His soul thine own will know at sight,
With him thy heart can speak outright.
Greet him nobly, love him well,
Show him where your best thoughts dwell,
Trust him greatly and for aye;
A true friend comes but once your way.

* * * * *

If you would keep your friend, approach him with a telescope, never with the microscope.

—*Anon.*

It is one of the severest tests of friendship to tell your friend of his faults. If you are angry with a man, or hate him, it is not hard to go to him and stab him with words; but so to love a man that you cannot hear to see the stain of sin upon him, and to speak painful truth through loving words—that is friendship. But few have such friends. Our enemies usually teach us what we are, at the point of the sword.

—*Beecher.*

My friend is not perfect—no more I—and so we suit each other admirably.

—*Pope.*

I could not live without the love of my friends.

—*John Keats.*

* * * * *

It is a good thing to be rich, and a good thing to be strong, but it is a better thing to be beloved of many friends.

—*Euripides.*

If you would know how rare a thing a true friend is, let me tell you that to be a true friend a man must be perfectly honest.

—*Henry W. Shaw.*

If we would build on a sure foundation in friendship, we must love our friends for their sakes rather than for our own.

—*Charlotte Bronte.*

In friendship even thought meets thought ere from the lips it part, and each warm wish springs mutual from the heart.

—*Pope.*

* * * * *

I have sped by land and sea, and mingled with much people,
But never yet could find a spot unsunned by human kindness;
Some more, and some less; but, truly, all can claim a little:
And a man may travel through the world, and sow it thick with friendships.

—*Tupper.*

* * * * *

Love is the greatest of human affections, and friendship the noblest and most refined improvement of love.

—*South.*

* * * * *

Love is flower-like;
Friendship is like a sheltering tree.

—*S. T. Coleridge.*

* * * * *

Seek no friend to make him useful, for that is the negation of friendship; but seek him that you may be useful, for this is of friendship's essence.

—*Wallace.*

* * * * *

Much certainly of the happiness and purity of our lives depends on our making a wise choice of our companions and friends. Many people seem to trust in this matter to the chapter of accidents. It is well and right, indeed, to be courteous and considerate to every one with whom one is thrown in contact, but to choose them as real friends is another matter.... If our friends are badly chosen they will inevitably drag us down; if well they will raise us up.

—*Avebury.*

Not only does friendship introduce daylight in the understanding out of darkness and confusion of thoughts; it maketh a fair day in the affections from storm and tempests; in consultation with a friend a man tosseth his thoughts more easily; he marshalleth them more orderly; he seeth how they look when they are turned into words; finally, he waxeth wiser than himself; and that more by an hour's discourse than by a day's meditation.

—*Bacon.*

* * * * *

Nothing is more common than the name of friend; nothing is more rare than friendship.

—*Phaedrus.*

O, friendship! thou fond soother of the human breast, to thee we fly in every calamity.

—*Goldsmith.*

Of all felicities the most charming is that of a firm and gentle friendship. It sweetens our cares, dispels our sorrows, and counsels us in all our extremities.

—*Seneca.*

Old friends are the greatest blessings of one's later years.

—*Horace Walpole.*

Of all the best things upon earth, I hold that a faithful friend is the best.

—*Owen Meredith.*

* * * * *

Reprove your friends in secret, praise them openly.

—*Publius Syrus.*

True friendship purifies and exalts. A friend may be a second conscience.

—*J. Stalker.*

The greatest happiness in life is the conviction that we are loved, loved for ourselves, or rather loved in spite of ourselves.

—*Hugo.*

The fewer our friends become, the more let us love one another.

—*Benjamin Franklin.*

The surest bulwark against evil is that of friendship.

—*Yonge.*

* * * * *

The years have taught some sweet, some bitter lessons—
none wiser than this:
To spend in all things else, but of one's friends to be most miserly.

—*James Russell Lowell.*

The best mirror is an old friend.

—*Tennyson.*

True friendships are eternal.

—*Cicero.*

That two men may be real friends, they must have opposite opinions, similar principles, and different loves and hatreds.

—*Chateaubriand.*

There are very few friends with whom one can be intimate on all subjects. Discover the range of your intimacy with each friend and never go beyond it.

—*J. A. Spender.*

* * * * *

Two persons will not be friends long if they cannot forgive each other's little failings.

—*La Bruyere.*

There is this important difference between love and friendship: while the former delights in extremes and opposites, the latter demands equalities.

—*Mme. de Maintenon.*

There is no folly equal to that of throwing away friendship, in a world were friendship is so rare.

—*Bulwer-Lytton.*

The very ground and gist of a noble friendship is the cultivation in common of the personal inner lives of those who partake in it, their mutual reflection of souls and joint sharing of experience inciting them to a constant betterment of their being and their happiness.

* * * * *

Think of the importance of friendship in the education of men. It will make a man honest; it will make him a hero; it will make him a saint. It is the state of the just dealing with the just, the magnanimous with the magnanimous, the sincere with the sincere, man with man.

—*Thoreau.*

There are two elements that go to the composition of friendship—truth and tenderness.

—*Emerson.*

There are a thousand nameless ties,
  Which only such as feel them know;
Of kindred thoughts, deep sympathies,
  And untold fancy spells, which throw
O'er ardent minds and faithful hearts
  A chain whose charmed links so blend,
That the light circlet but imparts
  Its force in these fond words, *My friend.*

—*Mrs. Dinnies.*

* * * * *

We talk of choosing our friends, but friends are self-elected.

—*Emerson.*

Wanting to have a friend is altogether different from wanting to be a friend. The former is a mere natural human craving, the latter is the life of Christ in the soul.

—*J. R. Hitter.*

Whoever undertakes a friend's great part,
Should be renewed in nature, pure in heart,
Prepared for martyrdom, and strong to prove
A thousand ways the force of genuine love.

—*Cowper.*

A faithful friend is the true image of the Deity.

—*Napoleon.*

* * * * *

As I love nature, as I love singing birds, and gleaming stubble, and flowing rivers, and morning, and evening, and summer, and winter, I love thee, my friend.

—*Thoreau.*

* * * * *

A poet might sing you his sweetest of songs,
  But this must the poet have known:
Of the heart whose love to you only belongs,
Whose strength would be spent to save you from wrongs
Of a soul knit to yours with the mightiest thongs,
  And sing them for you alone!

An artist might paint you a picture fair;
  That would equal the greatest known;
But the heart of a friend, to do and to dare,
To save you from sorrow, and trial, and care,
Is something an artist, paint he ever so rare,
  Has never on canvas shown!

* * * * *

Ancient Menander accounted him happy that had but met the shadow of a true friend; verily he had reason to say so, especially if he had tasted of any; for truly, if I compare all the rest of my fore-passed life, which, although I have, by the mere mercy of God, passed at rest and ease, and except the loss of so dear a friend, free from all grievous affliction, with an ever quietness of mind, as one that have taken my natural and original commodities in good payment, without searching any others; if, as I say, I compare it all unto the four years I so happily enjoyed the sweet company and most dear society of that worthy man, it is nought but a vapor, nought but a dark and irksome light.

I do but languish, I do but sorrow; and even those pleasures all things present me with, instead of yielding me comfort, do but redouble the grief of his loss. We were co-partners in all things. All things were with us at half; methinks I have stolen his part from him. I was so accustomed to be ever two, and so inured to be never single, that methinks I am but half myself.

—*Montaigne.*

* * * * *

A friend's bosom
Is the inmost cave of our own mind

Where we sit from the wide gaze of day
And from the all-communicating air.

—*Shelley.*

* * * * *

A generous friendship no cold medium knows,
Burns with one love, with one resentment glows;
One should our interests and our passions be,
My friend must hate the man that injures me.

—*Pope.*

* * * * * A friend should bear his friend's infirmities.

—*Shakespeare.*

* * * * *

Be yourself, simple, honest, and unpretending, and you will enjoy through life the respect and love of friends.

—*Sherman.*

* * * * *

Do not trouble yourself much to get new things, whether clothes or friends. Turn the old; return to them.

—*Thoreau.*

* * * * *

A man can scarce allege his own merits with modesty, much less extol them; a man cannot sometimes brook to supplicate or beg; and a number of the like; but all these things are graceful in a friend's mouth which are blushing in a man's own.

—*Bacon.*

* * * * *

Come, friend, my fire is burning bright,
A fire's no longer out of place,
How clear it glows (there's frost tonight)

It looks white winter in the face.

Be mine the tree that feeds the fire,
Be mine, the sun knows when to set,
Be mine, the months when friends desire
To turn in here from cold and wet,

—*Constable.*

* * * * *

Eternal blessings crown my earliest friend,
And round his dwelling guardian saints attend;
Blest be that spot where cheerful guests retire
To pause from toil, and trim their evening fire;
Blest that abode where want and pain repair,
And every stranger finds a ready chair:
Blest be those feasts with simple plenty crowned,
With all the ruddy family around.

—*Goldsmith.*

* * * * *

But let us drink a merry toast,
Let's drink to now and here,
Good fellowship shall be our boast,
In either woe or cheer!
O'er joys we've had, why sorrow brew?
Why live in days gone past?
We'll drink to friends both old and new,
Just so our friends are fast.

—*Delaney.*

* * * * *

But oh, if grief thy steps attend,
If want, if sickness, be thy lot,
And thou require a soothing friend,

Forget me not! Forget me not!

—*Opie.*

* * * * *

We just shake hands at meeting
With many that come nigh;
We nod the head in greeting
To many that go by.
But welcome through the gateway
Our few old friends and true;
The hearts leap up and straightway
There's open house for you,
Old friends,
There's open house for you.

—*Massey.*

* * * * *

Beyond all wealth, honor, or even health, is the attachment we form to noble souls; because to become one with the good, generous, and true, is to become in a measure good, generous, and true ourselves.

—*Arnold.*

* * * * *

Be slow in choosing a friend, slower in changing.

—*Franklin.*

* * * * *

Convey thy love to thy friend, as an arrow to the mark, to stick there; not as a ball against the wall to rebound back to thee.

—*Francis Quarles.*

* * * * *

Ah, friend, let us be true
To one another! For the world which seems
To lie before us like a land of dreams,

So various, so beautiful, so new,
Hath really neither joy, nor love, nor light,
Nor certitude, nor peace, nor help for pain;
And we are here as on a darkling plain
Swept with confused alarms of struggle and flight,
Where ignorant armies clash by night.

—*Matthew Arnold.*

* * * * *

Friendship is power and riches a11 to me;
Friendship's another element of life;
Water and fire are not of more general use
To the support and comfort of the world
Than friendship to the being of my joy;
I would do everything to serve a friend.

—*Southerne.*

* * * * *

For every leaf the loveliest flower,
Which beauty sighs for from her bower—
For every star a drop of dew—
For every sun a sky of blue—-
For every heart, a heart as true.

—*Bailey.*

* * * * *

Friendship receives its crown in marriage when love is mingled with admiration and respect.

* * * * *

Friendship, one soul in two bodies.

—*Pythagoras.*

* * * * *

Friendship! mysterious cement of the soul!
Sweet'ner of life, the solder of society!
I owe thee much. Thou hast deserved of me
Far, far beyond whatever I can pay.
Oft have I proved the labors of thy love,
And the warm efforts of the gentle heart
Anxious to please. O! when my friend and I
In some thick wood have wander'd heedless on,
Hid from the vulgar eye, and sat us down
Upon the sloping cowslip-covered bank,
Where the pure limpid stream has slid along,
In grateful errors through the under-wood,
Sweet murmurings, methought the shrill-tongued thrush
Mended his song of love; the sooty blackbird
Mellow'd his pipe, and soften'd every note;
The eglantine smell'd sweeter, and the rose
Assumed a dye more deep.
O! then the longest summer's day
Seem'd too, too much in haste: still the full heart
Had not imparted half: 'tis happiness
Too exquisite to last!

—*Blair.*

* * * * *

Friendship was given us by nature as the handmaid of virtues, and not as the companion of our vices.

—*Cicero.*

* * * * *

Friendships, like trees, bring forth fruit after their kind. Corrupt friendships, corrupt fruit; good friendship, good fruit.

—*Diggle.*

* * * * *

Friendship is usually treated by the majority of mankind as a tough and everlasting thing which will survive all manner of bad treatment. But this is an exceedingly great and foolish error; it may die in an hour of a single unwise word.

—*Ouida.*

* * * * *

Friendship is a vase, which when it is flawed by heat, or violence, or accident, may as well be broken at once; it can never be trusted after. The more graceful and ornamental it was, the more clearly do we discern the hopelessness of restoring it to its former state. Coarse stones, if they are fractured, may be cemented again; precious ones never.

—*Walter Savage Landor.*

* * * * *

Hand grasps hand, eye lights eye, in good Friendship.
And great hearts expand and grow one in the sense of this world's
life.

—*Browning.*

* * * * *

God never loved me in so sweet a way before;
'Tis he alone who can such blessings send;
And when His love would new expression find
He brought thee to me and He said, "Behold a friend."

* * * * *

Friendship is the wine of existence; love the dram-drinking.

—*Bulwer.*

* * * * *

He who has ceased to enjoy his friend's superiority, has ceased to love him.

—*Madame Swetckine.*

* * * * *

I thank Thee, Lord, for every moment dropped
Into my life that had some sweetness in it,
For all the golden hours when friendship met
And gave up heart for heart and thought for thought,
For all the love that faithful hearts let fall,
To drop into mine own; for every look
From loving eyes; for every smile or word
That gladdened me; for subtle influence
That made me strong, dear Lord, I thank Thee.

—*Pastor.*

* * * * *

I breathed a song into the air,
It fell to earth, I knew not where;
For who has sight so keen and strong,
That it can follow the flight of a song;

* * * * *

The song from beginning to end,
I found again in the heart of a friend.

—*Longfellow.*

* * * * *

I find no place that does not breathe
Some gracious memory of my friend.

—*Tennyson.*

* * * * *

I awake this morning with devout thanksgiving for my friends, the old and the new.

—*Emerson.*

* * * * *

I can only urge you to prefer friendship to all human possessions; for there is nothing so suited to our nature, so well adapted to prosperity or adversity.

—*Cicero.*

* * * * *

If any little love of mine
  May make a life the sweeter,
If any little care of mine
  May make a friend's the fleeter,
If any life of mine may ease
  The burden of another,
God give me love and care and strength
  To help my toiling brother.

* * * * *

If you have a friend worth loving,
Love him. Yes, and let him know
That you love him, ere life's evening
Tinge his brow with sunset glow;
Why should good words ne'er be said
Of a friend till he is dead?

—*Unknown.*

Old books, old wine, old Nankin blue,
All things, in short, to which belong
The charm, the grace that Time makes strong—
All these I prize, but (*entre nous*)
  Old friends are best!

—*Austin Dobson.*

* * * * *

I never crossed your threshold with a grief
  But that I went without it, never came
  Heart hungry but you fed me,

And gave the sorrow solace and relief.

I never left you but I took away
The love that drew me to your side again,
Through the wide door that never could remain
Quite closed between us for a little day.

* * * * *

If you would be loved as a companion, avoid unnecessary criticism.

—*Sir Arthur Helps.*

* * * * *

If you have friends in adversity, stand by them.

—*Dickens.*

* * * * *

It is every man's duty to make himself profitable to mankind.

—*Seneca.*

* * * * *

If a man should importune me to give a reason why I loved him, I find it could no otherwise be expressed than by making answer: because it was he, because it was I.

—*Montaigne.*

* * * * *

Indifferent people can only wound you in heterogeneous parts, maim you in your arm or leg: but the friend can make no pass but at the heart itself.

—*Steele.*

* * * * *

Tell me, gentle traveler, who hast wandered through the world, and seen the sweetest roses blow, and brightest gliding rivers, of all thine eyes have seen, which is the fairest land? "Child, shall I tell thee where nature is more blest and fair? It is where those we love abide. Though that space be small, ample is it above kingdoms; though it be a desert, through it runs the river of Paradise, and there are the enchanted bowers."

—*Unknown.*

* * * * *

My coat and I live comfortably together. It has assumed all my wrinkles, does not hurt me anywhere, has moulded itself on my deformities, and is complacent to all my movements, and I only feel its presence because it keeps me warm. Old coats and old friends are the same thing.

—*Hugo.*

* * * * *

Judge not thy friend until thou standest in his place.

—*Rabbi Hillel.*

* * * * *

Let no man think he is loved by any man when he loves no man.

—*Epictetus.*

* * * * *

My friend peers in on me with merry
  Wise face, and though the sky stay dim,
The very light of day, the very
  Sun's self comes in with him.

—*A. C. Swinburne.*

* * * * *

O sweeter than the honey well,
  Deep in the sweetest rose of June,
And all sweet things the tongue can tell
  On clover-scented afternoon,
Is friendship that has lived for years
Through fortune, failure, and through tears.

Though he who wears it sacredly
  Be swarted like the rafters are
That shelter him, eternity
  May hold few jewels half so rare!
And God will find for such a friend
Some sweeter slumber in the end.

—*Botsford.*

* * * * *

Still, Love a summer sunrise shines,
  So rich its clouds are hung,
  So sweet its songs are sung.
And Friendship's but broad, common day,
  With light enough to show
  Where fruit with brambles grow;
  With warmth enough to feed
  The grain of daily need.

—*Unknown.*

* * * * *

Only—but this is rare—
  When a beloved hand is laid in ours,
When jaded with the rush and glare
  Of the interminable hours,
Our eyes can in another's eyes read clear,
When our world-deafened ear
Is by the tones of a loved voice caressed—
A bolt is shot back somewhere in our breast,
And a lost impulse of feeling stirs again.
The eye sinks inward, and the heart lies plain,
And what we mean, we say, and what we would, we know.

—*Arnold.*

* * * * *

Yes, we must ever be friends; and of all who offer you friendship,
Let me be the first, the truest, the nearest, the dearest.

—*Longfellow.*

* * * * *

The only danger in friendship is that it may end.

—*Thoreau.*

* * * * *

Of all the heavenly gifts that mortal men commend,
What trusty treasure in the world can countervail a friend?
Our health is soon decayed; goods, casual, light and vain;
Broke have we seen the force of power, and honor suffer stain.
In body's lust man doth resemble but base brute;
True virtue gets and keeps a friend, good guide of our pursuit.
Whose hearty zeal with ours accords in every case;
No term of time, no space of place, no storm can it deface.

—*Nicholas Grimoald.*

* * * * *

When we have fallen through story after story of our vanity and aspiration, and sit rueful among the ruins, then it is that we begin to measure the stature of our friends; how they stand between us and our own contempt, believing in our best.

—*Stevenson.*

* * * * *

Reason is the torch of friendship, judgment its guide, tenderness its aliment.

—*De Bonald.*

* * * * *

Some I remember and will ne'er forget
My early friends, friends of my evil day;
Friends in my mirth, friends in my misery too,
Friends given by God in mercy and in love;

My counsellors, my comforters, and guides;
My joy in grief, my second bliss in joy;
Companions of my young desires; in doubt
My oracles; my wings in high pursuit.
Oh, I remember, and will ne'er forget
Our meeting spots, our chosen sacred hours;
Our burning words that utter'd all the soul;
Our faces beaming with unearthly love;
Sorrow with sorrow sighing, hope with hope
Exulting, heart embracing heart entire.

—*R. Pollok.*

* * * * *

Some love the glow of outward show,
  Some love mere wealth, and try to win it;
The house to me may lowly be,
  If I but like the people in it!

What's all the gold that glitters cold,
  When link'd to hard or haughty feeling?
Whate'er we're told, the nobler gold
  Is truth of heart and manly dealing!

Then let them seek, whose minds are weak,
  Mere fashion's smile, and try to win it;
The house to me may lowly be,
  If I but like the people in it!

—*Swain.*

* * * * *

Talk not of wasted affection,
Affection never was wasted;
If it enrich not the heart of another,
Its waters returning
Back to their springs like the rain,
Shall fill them full of refreshment;
That which the fountain sends forth

Returns again to the fountain.

—*Longfellow.*

* * * * *

There is no greater bane to friendship than adulation, fawning, and flattery. For this vice should be branded under as many names as possible, being that of worthless and designing men, who say everything with a view of pleasing, and nothing with regard to truth. Now while hypocrisy in all things is blamable (for it does away with all judgment of truth, and adulterates truth itself), so especially is it repugnant to friendship, for it destroys all truth, without which the name of friendship can avail nothing.

—*Cicero.*

* * * * *

These things do not require to be spoken; there is something in the hand grip and the look in the eye that makes you know your man.

—*Chambers.*

* * * * *

The man who prefers his dearest friend to the call of duty will soon show that he prefers himself to his dearest friend.

—*Robertson.*

* * * * *

There is nothing like putting the shine on another's face to put the shine on our own. Nine-tenths of all loneliness, sensitiveness, despondency, moroseness, are connected with personal interests. Turn more of those selfish interests into unselfish ones, and by so much we change opportunities for disheartenment into their opposite. By a law of Nature part of her beautiful economy, he who lives most for others is really living most for himself.

—*Gannett.*

* * * * *

The foundation of that steadfastness and constancy which we seek in friendship, is sincerity. For nothing is steadfast which is insincere.

—*Cicero.*

* * * * *

The wise man seeks a friend in whom are those qualities which he himself may lack; for thus being united is their friendship the more completely defended against adversity.

—*Jeremy Taylor.*

* * * * *

The Swallow is a summer bird;
He in our chimneys, when the weather
Is fine and warm, may then be heard
Chirping his notes for weeks together.

Come there but one cold wintry day,
Away will fly our guest the Swallow:
And much like him we find the way
Which many a gay young friend will follow.

In dreary days of snow and frost,
Closer to Man will cling the Sparrow:
Old friends, although in life we're crost,
Their hearts to us will never narrow.

Give me the bird—give me the friend—
Will sing in frost—will love in sorrow—
Whate'er mischance to-day may send,
Will greet me with his sight to-morrow.

—*Lamb.*

* * * * *

True happiness consists not in the multitude of friends, but in the worth and choice. —*Dr. Johnson.*

* * * * *

The earth-born clod who hugs his idol pelf,
His only friends are Mammon and himself;
The drunken sots, who want the art to think,
Still cease from friendship when they cease from drink.
The empty fop who scarce for man will pass,
Ne'er sees a friend but when he views his glass.
Friendship first springs from sympathy of mind,
Which to complete the virtues all combine,
And only found 'mongst men who can espy
The merits of his friend without envy.
Thus all pretending friendship's but a dream,
Whose base is not reciprocal esteem.

—*Allan Ramsay.*

* * * * *

We grow by love. It is said, why live for others? But others are our nutriment.

—*Channing.*

* * * * *

There are no rules for friendship. It must be left to itself. We cannot force it any more than love.

—*Hazlitt.*

* * * * *

There are few subjects which have been more written upon, and less understood, than that of friendship. To follow the dictates of some, this virtue instead of being the messenger of pain becomes the source of every inconvenience. Such specialists, by expecting too much from friendship, dissolve the connection, and by drawing the bands too loosely at length break them. It is certain that the best method to cultivate this virtue, is by letting it, in some measure, make itself; a similitude of minds and of studies, and even sometimes a diversity of pursuits, will produce all the pleasures that arise from it. The current of tenderness widens as it proceeds; and two men imperceptibly find their hearts filled with good nature for each other, when they were at first only in pursuit of mirth or relaxation.

—*Oliver Goldsmith.*